DISNEY'S

THE
LION KING

The Flamingos Are Tickled Pink

A Book of Idioms

by **Chip Lovitt**

illustrated by **Marshall Toomey** and **H. R. Russell**

DISNEY PRESS

NEW YORK

Library of Congress Catalog Card Number: 94-79214
ISBN: 0-7868-3036-0
FIRST EDITION
1 3 5 7 9 10 8 6 4 2

I'm Zazu the hornbill, and here's the morning report. I don't have a script, so I'll just go out on a limb and wing it.

Simba wants to follow in the
footprints of his father, King Mufasa,
but he keeps coming up a little short.

The giraffes have their heads in the clouds—except for one who's under the weather.

The turtles are shy,
but they're slowly
coming out of their shells.

The bees are making a
beeline for the honey.

Timon thinks Pumbaa
eats like a pig, but
Pumbaa swears he's
turning over a new leaf.

The anteaters are tongue-tied.

The hyenas were hungry, but they just laughed it off.

The flamingos are tickled pink, and
the parrots are green with envy.

The snakes are completely
wrapped up in themselves.

The baboons are going bananas, and the monkeys are really getting into the swing of things.

The hippos are making a big splash—
except for one who's being
a real stick-in-the-mud.

The warthogs like to hog all the space at the water hole, but the antelope keep horning in.

The elephants have
their noses out of joint.

The fish always go with the flow.

As far as the big news goes,
that ought to fit the bill.
I guess you could say
it's a jungle out there!